VICTORIA WOODHULL

VICTORIA WOODHULL

Fearless Feminist

Kate Havelin

Twenty-First Century Books/Minneapolis

This book is for my mother, my sisters, my friends—for all the strong women with whom I have had the chance to live, work, protest, run, and laugh.

Twenty-First Century Books
A division of Lerner Publishing Group
241 First Avenue North
Minneapolis, MN 55401 U.S.A.

Website address: www.lernerbooks.com

Library of Congress Cataloging-in-Publication Data

Havelin, Kate, 1961–
Victoria Woodhull / by Kate Havelin.
p. cm. — (Trailblazer biographies)
Includes bibliographical references and index.
ISBN-13: 978–0–8225–5986–3 (lib. bdg. : alk. paper)
ISBN-10: 0–8225–5986–2 (lib. bdg. : alk. paper)
1. Woodhull, Victoria C. (Victoria Claflin), 1838–1927—Juvenile literature. 2. Feminists—United States—Biography—Juvenile literature. 3. Suffragists—United States—Biography—Juvenile literature. 4. Presidential candidates—United States—Biography—Juvenile literature. 5. Presidents—United States—Election—1872—Juvenile literature. I. Title. II. Trailblazer biography.
HQ1413.W66H38 2007
305.42'092—dc22 2005022824

Manufactured in the United States of America
1 2 3 4 5 6 – JR – 12 11 10 09 08 07

Contents

Introduction: A Woman Ahead of Her Time

Crowds packed New York City's Cooper Institute auditorium in January 1873. They were waiting to hear the most controversial woman in the country. Law enforcement officers were at the lecture hall as well. They waited to arrest Victoria Woodhull if she showed up to give her talk called "The Naked Truth."

Suddenly a woman, bundled in a shawl, her head covered with a scarf, moved toward the podium. Once there, the woman removed the shawl and scarf and stood before the thousand people jammed in the hall. Victoria Woodhull was ready to dazzle her audience. She spoke for more than an hour about justice and how society needed to be changed. After the lecture, as the crowd applauded, Woodhull stepped forward. She extended her arms so that the police could handcuff her. Then she left the stage, under arrest again.

Victoria Woodhull is not widely known, but the list of her achievements is historic. She was the first woman to run for U.S. president. She and her sister

Tennessee (nicknamed Tennie) were the first women stockbrokers in the nation. They traded stock on New York City's Wall Street. And Victoria and Tennie were among the first American women to own and run a weekly newspaper.

Victoria Woodhull was ahead of her time. She fought fiercely for women's rights and workers' rights. She was a suffragist—someone who believed women deserved the right to vote. She believed

An etching of a confident Victoria Woodhull from the 1800s. Defying economic, social, and gender norms, Woodhull was a vocal activist for women's and workers' rights.

that women should have the right to control their bodies and their lives. She talked about birth control when few others dared even to say the words aloud. She also spoke in support of labor unions (groups that stand up for workers' rights).

With a life story that would make a blockbuster movie—rich with adventure, suffering, love, and bravery—Victoria Woodhull became a celebrity of her day. She drew huge audiences at lectures around the country. Copies of her photograph were popular items. The day she and Tennie opened their Wall

Woodhull *(front left)* demands her right to vote in a New York state election in 1871. She further challenged U.S. political law, running for president in 1872.

Street brokerage (stock exchange business), four thousand people lined up outside the sisters' office. Some were potential customers—but many were merely curious. Newspapers ran endless stories about "the Bewitching Brokers." It would be a century before another woman would own a brokerage.

In 1872 Victoria Woodhull ran for president of the United States. She competed against the popular incumbent (current president running for reelection), Ulysses S. Grant. But it would take another forty-eight years for women to win the right to vote—one of the most powerful rights of U.S. citizens. And more than a century after Woodhull was nominated for president, no woman has yet been elected to the White House.

On election day 1872, Ulysses Grant easily won re-election. Woodhull was in jail, charged with sending obscene (indecent) material through the mail. By the time she was jailed, Woodhull had lost her Wall Street fortune. For a brief time, she was homeless. Woodhull and her family seemed doomed to poverty. But Victoria Woodhull's story wasn't over. She would gain another fortune, in another country.

In 2002 Victoria Woodhull was entered into the National Women's Hall of Fame. Yet if she were alive in modern times, the views she voiced in 1872 would still outrage many people.

She was truly a woman ahead of her time.

Victoria Woodhull was named after Great Britain's Queen Victoria *(sitting on throne above).* Queen Victoria ruled from 1837 to 1901.

Chapter One
A Hard Start

The one-story house in Homer, Ohio, was run-down and rickety. Neighbor kids ran back and forth over the porch to hear the boards rattle. In that plain house, on September 23, 1838, Annie Claflin gave birth to her seventh child. She named the baby Victoria, in honor of the eighteen-year-old British queen who had been crowned earlier that year.

Victoria would say later that being named after an important woman leader was a good sign. She called it "a favoring omen." But the times Victoria Claflin was born into were anything but favorable. The United States had just gone through an economic panic—a period when many people lost their jobs and had little money. An even longer and more serious financial crisis, called an economic depression, would hit in 1839.

To support his growing family, Victoria's father, Buck, tried many jobs. He worked in taverns and as a laborer transporting lumber. But much of what Buck Claflin did to earn money was against the law. He stole horses. He cheated. Not surprisingly, many of Homer's four hundred residents did not approve of Buck's scams. The neighbors did not like Annie's housekeeping much, either. She didn't believe in having curtains, for example.

In 1841 Buck and Annie ended up losing the little bit of land they owned. All they had left was an unused gristmill to grind grain and their unpainted wooden house. The family struggled to survive. Some of the children had to beg for food. Victoria went to her neighbors, the Scribners, and asked if they had any little jobs she could do to earn money. Twenty-one-year-old Rachel Scribner befriended young Victoria. But one day, when Victoria was about five years old, she went next door and learned that Rachel had fallen ill suddenly and died. Upset, Victoria went to a nearby orchard. Looking up, she saw a vision of her dead friend. Victoria saw Rachel take her hand and glide through the air with her. Victoria went home and told her mother, "I had been among the angels."

Victoria likely heard a lot about angels and the spirit world from her mother. Annie believed in spirits, especially after two daughters, Delia and Odessa, died before Victoria was born. Like many people who lose loved ones, Annie looked to religion and the spiritual world for comfort. Annie began taking Victoria with her to religious prayer meetings. There, young Victoria learned the rhythm and language of preaching. Soon she was telling Bible stories to other children. "Sinners, repent!" Victoria would cry.

Life at home was rough. Victoria said later she had been "a child without a childhood." When she was still very young, she had to wash, cook, iron, and chop wood. She also helped care for her younger sisters, Tennessee and Utica. To make matters worse,

Victoria's mother, Annie, took her to prayer meetings *(above)* and services. Young Victoria took to religion, preaching to other children and warning them to stop sinning.

the girls' father drank too much alcohol. Buck used to beat his children with a braided whip of willow reeds. Sometimes Annie stopped him. Other times, she joined in. After one harsh whipping, Victoria's favorite brother, Hebern, ran away.

When she was eight, Victoria began attending school. She learned that she had a photographic memory—an ability to see something once and remember it clearly. But Victoria went to school for just three years. Even then she didn't attend regularly. Neither Buck nor Annie cared much about their children's education. And Buck had discovered that people would pay to hear Victoria speak. Traveling around Ohio with her father, Victoria preached to earn money. During her chaotic childhood, Victoria learned many lessons outside of school. She learned how to handle people and how to survive hard times.

Around 1853 Buck bought five hundred dollars worth of insurance on his old gristmill. If anything happened to the mill, Buck would receive money from the insurance company. Not long afterward, the mill burned down. The people of Homer suspected that Buck had started the fire himself to collect the insurance money. Buck had already left town, but Annie, Victoria, and six of her siblings were still in Homer. The Presbyterian church in Homer held a fund-raiser for the family. The townspeople gave Annie a horse-drawn wagon and supplies. Then they asked the Claflins to leave town.

In 1853 the members of the Presbyterian church in Homer, Ohio, took up a collection—enough for a wagon and some supplies—and sent the Claflins packing.

The family moved to Mount Gilead, Ohio. Victoria's older sister Maggie lived there with her husband. In Mount Gilead, Victoria, who was fourteen years old, and Tennie, who was about nine, began supporting the family as clairvoyants. Clairvoyants were believed to be able to see the future. People paid a dollar to have the young girls predict what lay ahead. When Victoria told her father she didn't know how to tell fortunes, his advice was brief: "Be a good listener, child."

While the Claflins were in Mount Gilead, Victoria got sick. Her family called a local doctor named Canning Woodhull. After Victoria recovered, the twenty-eight-year-old doctor invited the teenaged girl to the town's Fourth of July picnic. After the picnic, Canning told Victoria, "My little puss, tell your father and mother that I want you for a wife." On November 23, 1853, not long after Victoria's fifteenth birthday, the couple married. Victoria hoped that marriage would be an escape from the endless chores and responsibilities of a stressful home.

Married life, however, was no relief. Victoria quickly learned Canning was not a successful doctor. He had few patients and little money. He spent the money that he did earn on alcohol. Soon the young bride realized that her husband was addicted to drinking liquor. Victoria recalled the moment when she realized her husband was an alcoholic. "In a single day," she said, "I grew ten years older."

A year later, in December 1854, the couple was living in Chicago, Illinois. Victoria gave birth to her first child there. She named her baby boy Byron, after the famous English poet, Lord Byron. But the Woodhulls' firstborn would never write poetry. Byron was born developmentally delayed. He would never be able to speak clearly or communicate well. Victoria later said that, when she realized her son would not grow up like other children, "My heart was broken."

Chapter Two
On the Road, Struggling

In 1855 the couple and their young son moved to San Francisco. Gold had been discovered in California in 1848, and thousands of people had headed West, hoping to strike it rich. The Woodhulls didn't go to mine gold. But they, like many others, wanted a fresh start and a chance to make money. Life out west wasn't easy, though. Woodhull said that she and Canning were "beggars in a land of plenty."

In San Francisco, Woodhull took jobs sewing clothes. While working at a dressmaker's shop, she met an actress named Anna Cogswell. Cogswell encouraged the pretty young mother to try acting in plays. With her photographic memory, Woodhull quickly memorized her lines. Soon she was earning fifty-two dollars a week, a good amount of money at the time. But Woodhull didn't enjoy being an actress.

One night in 1857, Woodhull was performing in a play about two lonely brothers far from each other. Suddenly she saw her sister. Tennie was back East in Ohio, but Woodhull would later claim that Tennie told her, "Victoria, come home." Woodhull left the theater, still dressed in her stage costume, and packed her bags. The next morning, the Woodhulls and their son began the monthlong journey back East.

Woodhull's mother greeted her when the family arrived in Ohio. Annie said that she had told Tennie, "My dear, send the spirits after Victoria to bring her home." Annie and her daughters were among many Americans of their time who believed in spiritualism. Spiritualists thought that people could "talk" to one another even if they were thousands of miles apart. They also believed it was possible to communicate with dead people's spirits. Mediums are people who claim to have the power to communicate with the dead.

So many people wanted to communicate with dead loved ones that mediums could earn big money. Buck soon put Tennie to work as a medium. A Columbus, Ohio, newspaper ran an advertisement for "A WONDERFUL CHILD! MISS TENNESSEE CLAFLIN WHO IS ONLY FOURTEEN YEARS OF AGE!!" Tennie was sixteen, but Buck said she was younger so her powers would seem more impressive. He made Tennie work in a hotel room as a medium from eight in the morning until nine at night. For one dollar per person, Tennie told fortunes and communicated with the spirits of people dead or far away. Soon she was earning one hundred dollars a day. The Claflins also sold "Miss Tennessee's Magnetio Life Elixir for Beautifying the Complexion and Cleansing the Blood." The potion wasn't medicine. Instead, it was mostly alcohol. Eager to believe in cures, however, people paid two dollars a bottle for the elixir.

A medium *(front center)* tells fortunes during the 1800s. Tennie and Woodhull worked as mediums, telling people what they wanted to hear and separating them from their money.

"It was a hard life. I was forced to humbug [trick] people for the money," Tennie recalled.

Soon Woodhull was working as a medium alongside her younger sister. Woodhull, Tennie, and other Claflins began traveling to many cities. They told people's fortunes and promised to cure their diseases. On April 23, 1861, Woodhull was in New York. There she gave birth to her second child, a girl named Zula Maud. Canning helped deliver the baby—but then left mother and newborn alone. Both Woodhull and her baby were bleeding. Luckily, a neighbor came along and helped them. But Canning didn't come home for three days. Woodhull decided then that she would no longer live with her husband.

While Woodhull was leaving her husband, the eyes of the nation were focused on South Carolina.

Southerners there had opened fire on U.S. troops at Fort Sumter earlier in April. The Civil War (1861–1865) had begun. It would pit the South's Confederacy against the Union forces of the North. Many people assumed the war would last only a few months, but it dragged on for four years. More than six hundred thousand soldiers would die or be wounded. Countless families would turn to spiritualists in hopes of hearing from the loved ones they had lost.

When Woodhull was in Indianapolis, Indiana, young Byron became very sick with a high fever.

Hopeful sufferers visit a healer *(center)* during the 1800s. After her son Byron's illness, Woodhull came to believe that she, too, had miraculous healing powers.

Woodhull's mother, who was helping care for Byron, feared that he was dead. But Woodhull would not give up on her son. She held him close to her heart for hours—until, at last, he recovered. Woodhull was convinced that Byron's recovery meant that she had healing powers and could cause "miraculous cures" by touching people or listening to them. Woodhull came to believe that curing people was her purpose in life—her calling. She began working as a healer, trying to cure sick people with her "spiritual art."

Woodhull didn't want to cheat people. She wasn't trying to lie about her ability to heal. She even sewed the words from a biblical verse, Psalm 120, into the sleeve of her dress. The passage read, "Deliver my soul O Lord from lying lips and from a deceitful tongue." But not all spiritualists were as honest as Woodhull. Scams were common among healers and mediums. And scams were nothing new for Buck Claflin. He had spent his life cheating people. He would go to a new town and visit the cemetery to learn who had died and when. He also had what was called a Blue Book, containing information about families in different towns. Many mediums studied this book. They used its details to make it appear that they were reading people's minds.

Sometimes the Claflins and Woodhull got in trouble with local authorities. And sometimes they would have to leave town quickly after residents learned they were being cheated. But rather than getting out of the medium business, Buck expanded. He decided to offer medical cures.

In 1863 Buck rented an entire hotel in Ottawa, Illinois. He called himself the King of Cancers and advertised that Tennie was now helping people with cancer. He used one floor of the rented hotel as a clinic. The Claflins claimed they could cure cancer fast. They used lye, a strong chemical that they said killed the disease. In truth, the lye burned patients' skin.

In January 1864, Woodhull left the family's clinic in Ottawa. She moved to Chicago with her children and began advertising her "magnetic healing" powers. But she did not stay in Chicago very long. By April, Woodhull had moved to Saint Louis, Missouri.

In Saint Louis, Woodhull advertised herself as a medium named Madame Holland. One of her patients was Civil War veteran James Harvey Blood. The former Union colonel was the founder and president of the Saint Louis Society of Spiritualists. When Colonel Blood visited "Madame Holland," she went into a trance. She informed him that "his future destiny was to be linked with hers in marriage."

Later, Woodhull would say that she and Colonel Blood were "betrothed [engaged] on the spot." They decided to marry immediately. But there was one problem. Blood and Woodhull were each already married to other people. Blood soon left his wife and young daughter to be with Woodhull. He and Woodhull both took steps to divorce their spouses.

While Woodhull spent time with her fiancé, her family faced new problems. In June 1864, the local police raided the Claflin's hotel clinic. They found patients abandoned, in pain, and dying. The Claflins

For a price, tonics—often little more than flavored alcohol—promised miracle cures that they couldn't deliver. The Claflins took part in such medical quackery, offering a false cure for cancer.

had fled. Authorities charged them with nine crimes, ranging from disorderly conduct to medical fraud (often called quackery). Tennie faced the most serious charges. She was blamed for causing the death of at least one patient, Rebecca Howe, who died on June 7, 1864.

By the time authorities were ready to charge Tennie with the crime, she and the rest of her family had left Illinois. The Claflins knew how to stay one step ahead of the law. And they never went to court for the fake cancer cure. It's not clear exactly which states they visited when. In any case, over the next year or two, Tennie, her brother Hebern, and sometimes Victoria

Woodhull were all on the road together. The siblings traveled to Missouri, Arkansas, and Tennessee. In the state for which she was named, Tennie married a gambler named John Bartels, but she soon left him.

Meanwhile, Woodhull and Blood took the next step. In Dayton, Ohio, Blood paid a minister five dollars to marry them on July 12, 1866. But the marriage application was incomplete, and the minister never filed the paperwork. Officially, Woodhull and Blood were not married. But the two considered themselves joined.

It wasn't long before Tennie met up with Woodhull and her new husband. After the Civil War ended, the

Tennie Claflin *(left)* joined Victoria and her new husband, James Harvey Blood, to take their brand of spiritualism to New York City in the1860s.

government had begun cracking down on spiritualists who claimed to have healing powers. The sisters soon decided to focus on another side of spiritualism. Victoria, Tennie, Woodhull's children, and Victoria's new husband left the healing business behind. They headed to a new city—and a new start.

Chapter Three
New York, New Business

Delicate lettering decorated the fancy business cards. They read, "Mrs. Victoria Woodhull and Miss Tennie C. Claflin, Clairvoyants." The cards did not mention any medical powers. When the sisters moved to New York, they still advertised themselves as mediums. But they focused on their ability to communicate with the dead.

One man who was eager to connect with relatives he'd lost was Cornelius Vanderbilt. Vanderbilt was a New York multimillionaire. He longed to reach his mother, Phoebe Hand, and his favorite son, George Washington Vanderbilt. Vanderbilt was one of the sisters' first and most loyal customers. He gave them his business, and he also encouraged others to do the same. His advice was, "Do as I do, consult the spirits."

Fortunately for the sisters, many people listened to what Cornelius Vanderbilt had to say. He had enormous power and an ego to match. He named a train after himself and had his own portrait painted on the headlights. His picture also decorated his New York Central Railroad stock certificates. But the tough tycoon was impressed with the ambitious sisters.

Vanderbilt, who was seventy-five years old, supposedly began a romantic affair with Tennie Claflin. He was more than fifty years older than she was. After Vanderbilt's wife, Sophia, died in August 1868, Vanderbilt asked Tennie to marry him. But she had never divorced John Bartels. Claflin turned down Vanderbilt's proposal, but she stayed with him.

Although Vanderbilt was closer to Tennie than to Victoria, he helped both sisters with their business. They helped him in return. Victoria Woodhull was able to give him business tips, thanks to her friend Josie Mansfield. Mansfield was an actress. She had met Woodhull years earlier in San Francisco, and she now lived in New York. Mansfield also happened to be the girlfriend of Jim Fisk. Fisk was one of Vanderbilt's

This nineteenth-century editorial cartoon shows the heated business competition between Cornelius Vanderbilt *(left)* and competitor Jim Fisk *(right)*.

Woodhull *(left)* received inside business tips about Jim Fisk's dealings from friend Josie Mansfield *(right)*. Woodhull gave this information to Vanderbilt, who helped her in business.

business competitors. He and Vanderbilt both made money buying and selling stocks on Wall Street. But Mansfield told Woodhull about Fisk's business plans. Woodhull, in turn, passed the information to Vanderbilt, who could then buy the stocks Fisk wanted. Grateful to Woodhull for this business advantage, Vanderbilt gave the sisters advice and money for investing on Wall Street.

Along with the lessons in business, Victoria Woodhull was also learning about politics. Her husband, Colonel Blood, introduced her to ideas about women's rights, birth control, and other causes. She became a passionate suffragist, or a person working for women's right to vote. At the time, the Constitution gave the vote only to white men. But some women were working to gain voting rights.

In 1869 two women leaders—Susan B. Anthony and Elizabeth Cady Stanton—organized the National

Woman Suffrage Association. Woodhull went to Washington, D.C., that January for the group's national convention. She was excited about the chance for women to have power. Woodhull later wrote, "Visions of the offices I might one day hold danced before my imagination." She wasn't an official part of the convention, but she still managed to attract attention. *The Evening Star* newspaper called Woodhull "The Coming Woman." The reporter noted, "Mrs. W. possesses a commanding intellect, refinement, and remarkable executive ability, and will undoubtedly play a conspicuous part in such changes should they come."

Susan B. Anthony carries a banner that reads, "Failure Is Impossible! Votes for Women." Anthony, along with Elizabeth Cady Stanton, organized the National Woman Suffrage Association in 1869. Woodhull joined the suffrage movement after attending an association meeting that year.

Changes were coming. The suffrage movement was gaining power. But other changes loomed as well. On September 24, 1869, the stock market crashed. A rush of buying and selling had begun. This flurry of trading led to rapidly falling stock prices. The farther prices fell, the more investors panicked. They began selling all their stock for whatever money they could get—pushing prices down further. This frenzied day on Wall Street—called a panic—became known as Black Friday. Many people who invested in the stock market lost all their money. Some devastated Wall Street stockbrokers killed themselves when their businesses failed.

Panicked traders crowd the New York Stock Exchange trading floor in a flurry of buying and selling during the crash of 1869 on September 24, or Black Friday.

While many lost money during the 1869 crash, Woodhull earned enough to open a stock brokerage with Tennie on New York's prestigious Wall Street *(above)*. It was the first of its kind.

But as other investors sold stock, Victoria Woodhull did the opposite. Watching prices plunge, Woodhull decided to buy some of the inexpensive stock. Women were not allowed on Wall Street's trading floor. So Woodhull sat outside, sending men in with orders to buy. She and Vanderbilt were confident that the market would recover and that prices would rise. Their bet paid off. Woodhull later said proudly, "I came out a winner." She and Vanderbilt both made money that day. That winter Vanderbilt gave the sisters a check for seven thousand dollars.

The sisters used their money wisely. On February 5, 1870, Victoria and Tennie opened their own Wall Street brokerage business. They were the first American women to own and run a Wall Street brokerage. The press called the enterprising sisters "The Queens of Finance," "The Sensation of New York," and "The Bewitching Brokers."

Woodhull, Claflin & Company sparked enormous attention. Newspapers reported that four thousand people visited the sisters' office on opening day. The office featured a back entrance for women customers who might not feel comfortable doing business with men. The *New York Herald* noted that the crush of customers and curious public didn't faze the new business owners. As the reporter described the scene, "the ladies received their visitors with a coolness and an eye to business that drew forth the plaudits [praise] and the curses of old veterans." Tennie Claflin calmly told a reporter, "I think a woman is just as capable of making a living as a man." She went on, "I don't care what society thinks: I have not time to care. I don't go to balls or theaters. My mind is in my business and I attend to that solely."

The women did attend to business. But their partnership was not just a two-person operation. Colonel Blood's name wasn't part of the firm's title. But his training as an accountant made him a key part of the brokerage. He and the sisters signed a contract giving him a monthly salary of seventy-five dollars to manage the firm. He had an equal share of the profits and losses, as well. Blood also served as his wife's secretary, writing her personal letters since she had never learned graceful penmanship or punctuation.

But none of the many newspaper stories about the

women stockbrokers mentioned James Blood. All three partners seemed to understand that it made a better story to act as if no man had helped with their success. And Woodhull, Claflin & Company did become successful. Less than two years after arriving almost penniless in New York, Victoria Woodhull bragged to a reporter that she had earned seven hundred thousand dollars.

The businesswomen's accomplishments drew attention from other women, as well. Susan B. Anthony visited the sisters' office in spring 1870. Anthony profiled the sisters in a long article for the March 1870 issue of the *Revolution.* Anthony ran this suffrage newspaper with Elizabeth Cady Stanton. Anthony interviewed Tennie Claflin. At that point, Tennie had more experience talking to reporters than her sister did, and most people associated the brokerage firm with her. "These

Elizabeth Cady Stanton *(right)* and Susan B. Anthony reported Woodhull and Tennie's business success in the suffrage paper, the *Revolution.*

two ladies (for they are ladies) are determined to use their brains, energy, and their knowledge of business to earn them a livelihood," Anthony wrote. "This woman firm in Wall Street marks a new era."

New era or not, the rules still favored men. Woodhull and Claflin still weren't allowed on the stock market trading floor. Even socializing was more limited for women. The sisters once tried to get a table at Delmonico's, a popular restaurant where businessmen went to eat, drink, and talk. Owner Lorenzo Delmonico told them he couldn't seat women without a male escort. The sisters were not discouraged. Claflin boldly stepped out of the restaurant, called in their

Woodhull and Claflin challenged policy at New York City's popular business restaurant Delmonico's *(above).* They received a seat along with the restaurant's traditionally all-male clientele.

carriage driver, and got a table. "Now waiter," Woodhull said, "you may bring us tomato soup for three." Claflin and Woodhull seemed willing to break down any barrier.

On April 5, 1870, the sisters and Woodhull's children moved into an elegant home in an upper-class part of New York. Colonel Blood also moved in, along with Victoria and Tennie's sister Maggie and her family. In just two years, Victoria Woodhull and Tennie Claflin had gone from struggling spiritualists to famous businesswomen. Their world seemed rich with opportunity.

Chapter Four
Vote for Victoria!

The trailblazing women stockbrokers continued to draw attention. They drew so much that in April 1870, the *New York Herald* began running a series of Victoria Woodhull's articles. But Woodhull's goals went well beyond a journalism career. In her first *Herald* article, on April 2, 1870, Woodhull stated her intention to run for president. The headline blared: "THE COMING WOMAN. VICTORIA C. WOODHULL . . . TO RACE FOR THE WHITE HOUSE—WHAT SHE WILL AND WHAT SHE WON'T DO."

Woodhull used her article to explain why voters should consider her as a candidate. "While others argued the equality of woman with man, I proved it by successfully engaging in business," she wrote. "I boldly entered . . . politics and business and exercised the rights I already possessed. I therefore claim the right to speak for the . . . women of the country, and . . . I now announce myself as a candidate for the Presidency."

In spring 1870, anything seemed possible for Victoria Woodhull. She had been a girl from a poor, troubled family. She had struggled with an alcoholic husband and a disabled son. But she had transformed herself into a successful businesswoman. Woodhull

African American men cast votes for the first time in the United States during the late 1800s. Ratification of the Fifteenth Amendment to the Constitution granted African American men the right to vote. But that right was still denied to women.

was confident enough to run for president when her country did not even allow her to vote. Voting rights in the United States had just expanded. In March 1870, the Fifteenth Amendment to the Constitution gave African American men the right to vote. It was still only men, however, who could cast ballots in elections. But gender wasn't the only barrier to Woodhull's candidacy. She was thirty-one years old—four years younger than the minimum age for presidents according to the U.S. Constitution.

It's doubtful whether many people—especially men in positions of power—took Woodhull's candidacy seriously. As a *Herald* article put it, "Mrs. Woodhull offers herself in apparent good faith as a candidate, and perhaps has a remote impression, or rather hope, that she may be elected but it seems she is rather in advance of her time. The public mind is not yet educated to the pitch of universal women's rights."

But Woodhull did not let others' doubts stand in her way. Shortly after she announced her bid for the White House, she broke yet another barrier. Victoria and her sister became the first women in the United States to publish a weekly newspaper. The first issue of *Woodhull & Claflin's Weekly* went on sale May 14, 1870. The paper's logo brimmed with Woodhull's energy and ambition. "UPWARD AND ONWARD," it declared.

EQUAL RIGHTS
NATIONAL WOMAN'S PARTY, Washington, D. C.
The Star Still Shines!
Bill Of Rights Day

WOODHULL & CLAFLIN'S WEEKLY.
PROGRESS! FREE THOUGHT! UNTRAMMELED LIVES!

Woman's Journal
And Suffrage News

The Quaker Drug Co.
DRUGGISTS TO HIS MAJESTY—THE PEOPLE
Three Great Stores in Seattle

Woodhull & Claflin's Weekly (upper right) joined other suffrage and civil rights newspapers in print on May 14, 1870.

Publishing a newspaper was a big step for Woodhull and Claflin. But it also made good sense. Every major political party had its own paper, and newspapers were the main tools for communicating information of all kinds. Woodhull called the newspaper her "pet." It was her prime concern, while the brokerage interested her sister more. However, Tennie did sometimes sell ads for the *Weekly*. In addition, Colonel Blood wrote and did other newspaper jobs. Another man, named Stephen Pearl Andrews, also helped shape the newspaper.

That spring the *Herald* published a story explaining Woodhull's ideas about women's rights. Although the paper credited Victoria Woodhull with writing the article, she probably had help. The style of the story seemed more like the work of Stephen Pearl Andrews. The well-educated Andrews was helping build up Woodhull's image as a presidential candidate. Regardless of who wrote the articles, they gave *Herald* readers a sense of the issues Woodhull supported. And the articles were later reprinted in a book so that more people could learn about Woodhull.

In the fall of 1870, Woodhull's *Weekly* began running a series of reports about "Frauds in Existing and in Projected Railroads." Woodhull and her sister had gotten their start with money from one of the country's leading railroad businessmen. But they weren't afraid to report on people who made money illegally in the railroad industry—or any other industry, for that matter. The sisters' paper went on to investigate

Woodhull and Claflin took on the powerful and popular minister Henry Ward Beecher *(right)* in a story that ran in the *Weekly* on October 29, 1870.

the insurance industry, Wall Street, and other big money businesses. Their stories were part of a growing trend in journalism to uncover hidden crime and other problems in the United States.

On October 29, 1870, the *Weekly* printed a story about the country's most well known and popular preacher, Henry Ward Beecher. Beecher led Plymouth Congregational Church in New York. The whole Beecher family was famous. Henry's father and five of his brothers were preachers. Two of Henry's sisters, Catharine and Harriet, were popular writers. Another sister, Isabella Beecher Hooker, was active in the suffrage movement.

The *Weekly* headline shouted the news: "Henry Ward Beecher . . . Charged . . . With A Series of Falsehoods, Slander, Moral Cowardice and Other Conduct Unbecoming a Christian Minister." Victoria Woodhull's newspaper stories about the preacher were daring. He was famous, popular, and influential. Woodhull's words endangered his reputation—but also hers.

Chapter Five

Headed to Washington

By late fall 1870, Woodhull had set her sights on a bigger target than a preacher. She decided to focus her attention on the nation's capital. She moved into a hotel in Washington, D.C., so that she could speak to Congress about suffrage. Women had been working to win the vote since 1848. Some suffragists wanted each U.S. state to individually grant women the vote. Others worked to pass a sixteenth constitutional amendment granting all American women the right to vote. But Victoria Woodhull didn't think women needed a Sixteenth Amendment. She argued that the Constitution and previous amendments together gave U.S. women the right to vote.

Woodhull had one important ally who also believed that existing laws already gave women voting rights. Representative Benjamin Butler was one of the most powerful members of Congress. The November 19, 1870, *Weekly* explained Woodhull and Butler's philosophy. Woodhull argued that suffragists didn't need to push for a special amendment, since the Constitution stated that "the citizens of each state shall be entitled to the privileges . . . of citizens in the several states." Woodhull knew that Wyoming had given women there the right to vote in 1869. She believed that meant all women in the United States now had the right to vote. Woodhull also argued that women were full citizens under the Fourteenth Amendment. This amendment read, "All persons born or naturalized in the United States . . . are citizens of the United States." And since voting is a basic part of being a citizen, Woodhull said, women citizens had the right to vote.

On December 19, 1870, Woodhull asked Congress to officially give women the right to vote. Two days later, the Senate and the House of Representatives reviewed her women's voting plan. It seemed as if Congress would take Woodhull's suffrage views seriously. The next month, Woodhull got a chance to testify before the House Judiciary Committee (a committee of the U.S. House of Representatives).

January 11, 1871, marked the first time any woman spoke before a committee of Congress. Victoria Woodhull was nervous. The day was important to her and other suffragists. But most of the committee members chose to show up late for Woodhull's historic speech. She began her testimony before a nearly empty room. To make matters worse, Representative John Bingham, the House Judiciary Committee chairman, was not on the suffragists' side. Bingham began by telling Woodhull, "Madam you are not a citizen." Bingham had sponsored the Fourteenth Amendment, but he didn't think it applied to women. Woodhull then quoted the amendment and even

In this illustration, Woodhull delivers her women's voting plan to a congressional committee in January 1871.

Bingham had to agree that women did indeed qualify as citizens under the amendment.

Chairman Bingham, however, wasn't the only congressman who opposed Woodhull and women's rights. A reporter noted that one representative from Wisconsin "seemed to regard the whole thing as a good joke." But another representative noted that Woodhull made her arguments "in as good a style as any congressman could have done." The *New York Herald* wrote, "there is no disguising the fact that the women suffrage advocates are making headway in Washington."

Later that day, Woodhull repeated her speech to a friendlier audience—a women's rights convention. Woodhull was nervous about public speaking, and the importance of the occasion must have made her even more uneasy. Her fear showed. She looked tense and had trouble breathing. Her voice shook. Still, the suffragists seemed to think that Woodhull was a good person to have on their side. She had money and influence, and she had already made history by addressing a congressional committee. By the end of the convention, the suffragists had named Woodhull to the National Committee of Women. Woodhull then stayed on in Washington to take the committee's ideas to Congress.

Woodhull and other suffragists wanted Congress to hold public hearings on women's rights. Such hearings, held by both the House and the Senate, were often the first step in creating new laws. But the House refused to hold hearings. In fact, John Bingham helped pass a resolution (a formal statement) allowing Congress to ignore women's rights.

In addition, not all American women supported the suffragists. About one thousand women signed a petition asking Congress *not* to give women the vote. Among the women who opposed suffrage were wives of senators and representatives. Catharine Beecher also held this view. Catharine, like many other people, believed that women's place was at home, cooking and taking care of children. Catharine wrote books about domestic life and encouraged other women to let men be in charge. That included voting and controlling business and government.

WOODHULL & CLAFLIN'S
WEEKLY.

PROGRESS! FREE THOUGHT! UNTRAMMELED LIVES!

BREAKING THE WAY FOR FUTURE GENERATIONS.

VOL. 2—No. 14.—WHOLE No. 40. NEW YORK, FEBRUARY 18, 1871. PRICE TEN CENTS.

VICTORIA C. WOODHULL & TENNIE C. CLAFLIN

EDITORS AND PROPRIETORS.

CONTENTS OF THIS NUMBER.

	PAGE.
The Reports of the Judiciary Committee on the Woodhull Memorial	5
A Historical Picture; The Carpet Baggers' Frauds and Thefts in the South; To our Readers, etc.	6
Woman Suffragists Aroused	7
The Majority Report of the Judiciary Committee on the Woodhull Memorial Reviewed	8
Declaration and Pledge of the Women of the United States, as formally Proposed and Adopted by the Woman's Suffrage Convention	10
National Labor Union	11
The Felon's Dock	13
Victoria C. Woodhull Delivering her Address on Constitutional Equality before the Judiciary Committee of the House of Representatives of the United States, Jan. 11, 1871	16

TO

NEWSMEN AND POSTMASTERS

THROUGHOUT

The United States, Canada and Europe.

On account of the very extraordinary and widespread demand which has sprung up for THE WEEKLY since the exposure of the frauds and villainies which are practiced upon the people by iniquitous corporations having no souls, was

THE

Cosmo-Political Party.

NOMINATION FOR PRESIDENT OF THE U. S.,

IN 1872.

VICTORIA C. WOODHULL

SUBJECT TO

RATIFICATION BY THE NATIONAL CONVENTION.

Woodhull ran stories about her bid for the U.S. presidency on the front page of every issue of the *Weekly* starting in January 1871.

Still, despite heavy opposition, Woodhull continued her fight for women's rights. *Weekly* issues often included ideas that readers could use in support of women's suffrage. Over time, the *Weekly* sent out approximately five thousand copies of Woodhull's plan to win the vote. Woodhull intended her newspaper to be her best political advertisement. For months, starting in January 1871, Woodhull's declaration of her candidacy ran on page one.

At the May 1871 suffrage convention, Woodhull gave a bold "Great Secession Speech." She threatened the government with women's secession (separation from the country) and treason if women did not get the vote. At the convention, Woodhull also announced she was forming a new political party—the Cosmopolitical Party. Woodhull's political party supported rights for women and workers. Woodhull spoke out for an eight-hour workday and new tax laws. She also wanted to reorganize the country's school systems so that every child had the right to a good free education. In addition, the new party wanted to limit presidents to one term but give former presidents a permanent seat in the Senate.

Free love was another controversial issue that arose during the campaign. Woodhull supported free love—the idea that people had the right to love whom they wanted, when they wanted. Woodhull believed that people had the right to divorce, which was uncommon in her era. She thought that both men and women should have the power to decide whom they wanted to love and marry. Saying that someone supported free love, however, was one of the worst insults of the time. Although the phrase "free love" came from a poem about spiritual freedom, it had come to represent loose morals and people who opposed stable marriages. Woodhull's new party took stands on many issues, but newspaper headlines focused on only one small piece of the Cosmopolitical agenda. "FREE LOVE!" they shouted.

Whatever the reactions, Woodhull said what she believed. Even some people who disagreed with her ideas respected her for being true to her beliefs.

Noted editor Horace Greeley wrote in his *New York Tribune,* "We toss our hats in the air for Woodhull. *She* has the courage of her opinions! *She* means business. *She* intends to head a new rebellion, form a new constitution, and begin a revolution. . . ."

But some suffragists didn't want to be known as Woodhull's followers. The convention voted to approve Woodhull's ideas about suffrage. However, Susan B. Anthony and Elizabeth Cady Stanton argued privately over Woodhull's role in the suffrage movement. Stanton supported Woodhull, but worried that she wasn't focused enough on suffrage. Stanton didn't want women's rights mixed with other issues. Anthony worried that the rumors circulating about Woodhull and Claflin's personal lives would hurt the entire women's movement. For her part, Stanton didn't even want to hear the rumors. "In regard to all the gossip about Mrs. W. I have one reply to make to my gentlemen friends," she wrote. "When the men who make laws for us in Washington, can . . . declare themselves pure & unspotted from all the sins . . . then we will demand that every woman who makes a constitutional argument on our platform shall be as chaste [pure] as [the goddess] Diana. If all 'they say' is true, Mrs. Woodhull is better than nine tenths of the Fathers, Husbands, and Sons."

But rumors continued to swirl. In May 1871, details about Woodhull's complicated life made the front page. Woodhull's mother sued Colonel Blood, claiming that her son-in-law had tried to kill her. "He has threatened my life several times," Annie Claflin

This editorial illustration shows a court scene from the 1871 legal struggle between Woodhull *(left)* and her mother *(center)*.

testified. "One night last November he came into the house in Thirty-eighth Street and said he would not go to bed till he had washed his hands in my blood." Annie Claflin's charges were never proven true, but they still made headlines. So did other news that came out during the trial. Under oath, Woodhull said she lived with two men: her husband, James Blood, and also her former husband, Dr. Canning Woodhull. Canning Woodhull, she said, was an alcoholic and needed care. But the press and public were shocked that a woman would live with a man other than her current husband. The trial also raised doubts about whether Woodhull and Blood were legally married, since no record of their wedding could be found.

After the trial, Woodhull wrote to the *New York Times* defending her way of life. "Dr. Woodhull being sick, ailing and incapable of self-support, I felt it my duty to myself and to human nature that he should be cared for," she declared. "My present husband, Colonel Blood, not only approves of this charity, but co-operates in it. I esteem it one of the most virtuous acts of my life." Two days later, the *Times* ran another letter from Woodhull. This piece argued that women—especially those who spoke out in public—were held to a different, higher standard than men.

Woodhull defended her views on free love, as well. She said it was a "cure for the immorality" of married people who had sexual affairs with people they weren't married to. She wrote, "I know of one man, a public teacher of eminence [importance] who lives . . . with the wife of another public teacher of almost equal eminence." Some readers knew that she was talking about Henry Ward Beecher. Beecher was rumored to have had affairs with a number of women in his congregation. He supposedly was involved with Elizabeth Tilton. Elizabeth's husband, Theodore, was an editor at several religious newspapers and wrote many columns that were published under Beecher's name.

Theodore Tilton went to the *Weekly* offices to meet Woodhull. He told her she was the first person to say publicly what others whispered. Tilton wanted Woodhull to meet his wife. The three had dinner together, and Tilton told Woodhull that Elizabeth feared publicity about her affair with Beecher. Over time, Tilton and Woodhull became close. Each said

Theodore Tilton *(right)* found himself tangled in the Beecher-Woodhull media battle, after his wife Elizabeth was named as one of the women with whom the Reverend Beecher was having an affair.

later that they had an affair, although each also sometimes denied the affair. What is known is that the religious leader and the suffragist spent many hours together. Tilton began writing a biography about Woodhull.

Newspapers, too, continued to write about the lively woman who was running for president. She showed a *New York Sun* reporter an outfit she planned to wear once she was in the White House. The clothes—knee-length pants, blue stockings, tunic, and necktie—violated society's rules about what women could wear.

Women were not allowed to wear pants, let alone short pants. The reporter told her, "Mrs. Woodhull, if you appear on the streets in that dress the police will arrest you." But Woodhull seemed confident that she could do—and dress—as she pleased. She told the reporter, "When I am ready to make my appearance in this dress, no police will touch me."

All the attention Woodhull received cost her, however. Woodhull's landlord told her to move out of her comfortable home. She and her relatives began looking for a cheaper place to live. The sisters' stock brokerage was no longer bringing in much money, since traders had not been buying much stock lately. And Woodhull was spending more and more money on the suffrage movement.

Meanwhile, Woodhull's political interests continued to grow. By July 1871, she stood firmly in support of the rights of working people and labor unions.

Then, in August, Tennie Claflin announced that she too was running for office. She wanted to become the first woman member of Congress. But her bid wasn't serious. And it hurt her sister's chances by making Woodhull's presidential dreams also seem like a publicity stunt.

In September Theodore Tilton's glowing biography of Victoria Woodhull went on sale. Critics hated the book, which described Woodhull as a brave, soulful woman who could communicate with angels. Woodhull hoped the book, which emphasized her background as a medium, would bring her support from spiritualists around the country. She did find new supporters among spiritualists. But many others, including some suffragists, bashed the book.

Just after her biography came out, Woodhull spoke before two conventions of spiritualists. No candidate had worked for their vote before. With thousands of members, however, the spiritualists had the potential to be a bigger and more powerful group of voters than suffragists or unions. Woodhull succeeded in winning the hearts and political support of the spiritualists.

The woman in this editorial cartoon is asking to buy a "her-book" rather than a hymnbook (him-book). The cartoon reflects the growing popularity of Woodhull's message—publicized through the *Weekly* and her biography—among women.

Woodhull raises her hand in defiance at a New York polling station, demanding the right to vote. This illustration appeared in the November 25, 1871, issue of *Harper's Weekly.*

The American Association of Spiritualists even voted to make Woodhull president of their group.

On election day, November 7, 1871—a year before the presidential election—Woodhull, Claflin, and ten other suffragists marched to a polling place. They wanted to vote.

A sketch in the November 25, 1871, issue of *Harper's Weekly* re-created the scene at the polls. A few determined women, including Woodhull with her arm raised in protest, were surrounded by dozens of men. Election officials in top hats and a burly police officer stood guarding the ballot boxes. "By what right do you refuse to accept the vote of citizens of the United States?" Woodhull asked the judges. An election judge points to a copy of the New York Constitution, which read that all men have the right to vote. The women held small copies of the U.S. Constitution—but the election judges refused to allow the women to vote.

Chapter Six
Free Love and Costly Choices

Shortly after the suffragists were denied the vote, about three thousand people gathered at New York City's Steinway Hall to hear one of Victoria Woodhull's most controversial speeches. On November 20, 1871, she lectured about the "Principles of Social Freedom." She talked about women's right to be free to determine their lives. But again, what people remembered most was Woodhull's stance on free love. She had proudly stated, "Yes, I am a free lover!"

Woodhull said both men and women should have the freedom to love anyone they wanted. As she put it, "I have an inalienable, constitutional, and natural right to love whom I may, to love as long or as short a period as I can, to change that love every day I please! And with that right neither you nor any law you can frame have any right to interfere." Woodhull's free love speech angered many people who heard it or read about in the papers. The *Independent* said Woodhull spoke "with a mouthful of dirt." But within two days, Woodhull had received thirteen invitations to repeat the speech that everyone was talking about.

Woodhull soon returned to touring with her lecture, needing both the money and the publicity for her ongoing presidential campaign. She spoke in eleven cities in thirteen days. The *Pittsburgh Dispatch* called Woodhull the "most prominent woman of our time." She drew crowds and enemies. Still, Woodhull continued to stand up for her principles. And her paper continued to make history. In December the *Weekly* reprinted German philosopher Karl Marx's *Communist Manifesto.* Woodhull's paper was the first in United States to publish this work, which would become a historic theory. Marx believed that capitalism—the system of private ownership—would fail and that workers would eventually control the businesses they worked in.

Karl Marx *(right)* wrote the *Communist Manifesto*—his vision for economics and labor—in 1847. Although published in Great Britain in 1848, it was not printed in the United States until 1871, when Woodhull ran it in its entirety in the *Weekly.*

By winter 1872, Woodhull had a new speech, titled "The Impending Revolution," which took on the class system of rich and poor. The lecture hall was packed. People bought tickets for just fifty cents and sold them for ten dollars to people eager to hear the talk. Inside the hall, Woodhull launched her war against the rich, saying, "A Vanderbilt may sit in his office and manipulate stocks . . . in a few years, he amasses $50 million from the industries of the country, and he is one of the remarkable men of the age. But if a poor, half-starved child were to take a loaf of bread from his cupboard, to prevent starvation, she would be sent [to prison]." She asked her listeners, "Is it right that the millions should toil all their lives long, scarcely having comfortable food and clothes, while the few manage to control all the benefits?"

This time, the newspapers largely ignored Woodhull's speech, noting that she drew crowds but saying little about the talk itself or its topic. Two days later, the *New York Times* ran an editorial rejecting Woodhull completely. When she wrote a letter in her defense, the editors sent it back to her, saying, "We cannot possibly afford the space for your letter." Woodhull ran it in her own *Weekly.*

The February 17, 1872, *Harper's Weekly* ran a sketch by Thomas Nast, a popular political cartoonist, labeling Woodhull as "Mrs. Satan." Nast's cartoon shows Woodhull with devil's horns and vulturelike wings. Holding a sign saying "Be saved by Free Love," Woodhull is shown trying to lure an exhausted woman who is bent under the weight of a

This editorial cartoon ran in *Harper's Weekly* in 1872 and is critical of Woodhull's belief in free love. It casts Woodhull as a devil, trying to lure a woman burdened by the difficulties of marriage down the path of free love and independence.

drunken man and several young children. But the woman replies that she would "rather travel the hardest path of matrimony [marriage] than follow [Woodhull's] footsteps." The cartoon suggested that an evil Woodhull urged moral women to ignore their family responsibilities.

A few months later, Woodhull faced renewed attention and criticism about her life when her former husband, Canning Woodhull, died at the age of forty-eight. Newspapers reported that he was addicted to opium, as well as alcohol. Media also reported on Woodhull's financial struggles. The brokerage business was failing. Cornelius Vanderbilt's two-year commitment to help fund *Woodhull & Claflin's Weekly* had just ended. The newspaper cost three hundred dollars more each week than it brought in. Still, Woodhull wanted to keep the paper alive. Woodhull's landlord didn't want an infamous woman with money problems as a tenant. He tried to evict (throw out) her family from their home.

May 1872 was a critical time for Woodhull. The suffragists were again holding a convention, and Woodhull hoped they would support her bid to become the country's first woman president. Leading suffragists remained deeply divided over Woodhull. Elizabeth Cady Stanton supported Woodhull, but Susan B. Anthony still did not want suffrage to get mixed with other social issues such as divorce, free love, and workers' rights. In the end, the suffrage convention did not endorse (formally support) the controversial Woodhull.

A day after the suffragists snubbed Woodhull, she found new allies. Woodhull invited suffragists who supported her to New York City's Apollo Hall on May 10. More than 650 suffragists, spiritualists, and other advocates showed up to hear Woodhull.

When Victoria Woodhull walked onstage, the crowd at Apollo Hall cheered for a full five minutes. "Women waved their handkerchiefs and wept, men shouted themselves hoarse and perfect confusion prevailed," the *New York Sun* reported. The gathering was the kickoff for another new political party created by Woodhull. She called her new group the Equal Rights Party. The Equal Rights Party quickly nominated Victoria Woodhull as their candidate for president of the United States. It was the first time any political party had endorsed a woman for the White House. The 668 delegates from twenty-two states made history again later that day when they nominated Frederick Douglass for vice president. Douglass was a leading African American publisher and statesman. He was the first African American to be nominated for a presidential ticket. But Douglass was not at the Equal Rights Party convention, and when he learned he was their choice for vice president, he said no.

Douglass supported the current president, Ulysses Grant, who was a member of the Republican Party. But some Republicans didn't think Grant had done enough for African Americans and other oppressed people. Liberal Republicans broke away from their party. They wanted Horace Greeley to become president. Greeley, the respected editor of the *New York Tribune,* won the presidential nomination from both liberal Republicans and the Democratic Party. Even Theodore Tilton, who had written Woodhull's biography, backed Greeley. (Tilton hoped he would get Greeley's job if the newsman were elected president. Woodhull and Tilton ended their friendship after he endorsed Greeley.)

Woodhull now had a party's endorsement, but she didn't have money. Her husband came up with a new way to raise campaign funds. Supporters were encouraged to lend money to the campaign. If Woodhull were elected, the money would be repaid. Equal Rights delegates lent sixteen hundred dollars and pledged to give almost another five thousand dollars' worth. Woodhull was desperate to raise enough money to pay the necessary fees to place her name on ballots around the country. But her Equal Rights Party didn't have the resources that the bigger, more established Democrats and Republicans had, and Woodhull was unable to get her name on most states' ballots.

While she was worrying about raising enough money to get on the ballot, Woodhull was also looking

Horace Greeley *(left)* and Ulysses Grant *(right)* battle for the presidency in this 1872 editorial illustration based on the biblical story of David and Goliath. Greeley is shown as David taking on President Grant, a powerful Goliath. Woodhull and her party could not compete with the power of these men and their parties.

for a place to live. She and her family had been forced to move from their home. They spent several weeks camping out at their brokerage office. Then the office landlord tried to squeeze them out. He raised the rent by one thousand dollars and demanded that they pay the extra money immediately. Woodhull and Claflin scrambled to find a landlord who would lease them an office. But it seemed as though no landlord in New York wanted to help the infamous woman running for president. Eventually, Woodhull found a landlord willing to rent them a place to live. Woodhull paid the rent using donations from Equal Rights delegates. The house doubled as the party's headquarters and also as the brokerage office. Woodhull wasn't the only person facing money problems. The country had sunk into a recession—a time of economic slowdown when many people and businesses struggle to pay their bills. The recession caused roughly four thousand U.S. businesses to fail in 1872.

The search for housing was not the only stress in Woodhull's life. Her children suffered the consequences of her controversial stands. Zula, her eleven-year-old daughter, had to leave school because other children's parents didn't want them to be around her.

Woodhull's problems grew worse as spring turned to summer. On June 15, 1872, the *Weekly* announced that "Newsmen were being bribed to exclude it [the *Weekly*] from their stands." In the past, the newspaper had enjoyed decent circulation, with about twenty thousand readers. But by the end of June, the *Weekly* was forced to suspend publication. The recession was

Despite unfavorable odds, Woodhull continued her run for the presidency in 1872. This political cartoon from 1872 shows Woodhull speaking to supporters at a campaign rally.

partly to blame, but Woodhull thought her newspaper's failure was linked to her candidacy. "We have learned that so long as we merely talked and wrote, the people did not mind it," Woodhull wrote. But, she said, "immediately following the May convention [when Woodhull was nominated for president] every opposer to our program rose up in arms . . . and they left no means untried . . . we were . . . in two short months, completely ruined financially."

Woodhull blamed the men in charge of business and government for her financial collapse. She believed that those in power felt threatened because she wanted to change the system. She also accused other newspapers of not covering her story because they didn't want her to succeed.

By August, Woodhull was in court because of her debts. She told the judge that she had no money to pay bills and didn't even own the clothes she was wearing. The family was once again asked to move out. Woodhull was desperate. Hoping against hope, she turned to one of the most powerful people she knew—the Reverend Henry Ward Beecher.

"Dear Sir," she wrote Beecher. "Within the past two weeks I have been shut out of hotel after hotel. . . . Now I want your assistance. I want to be sustained in my position in the Gilsey House [a hotel] from which I am now ordered out, and from which I do not wish to go—and all of this simply because I am Victoria C. Woodhull, the advocate of social freedom. I have submitted to this persecution just so long as I can endure. My business, my projects, in fact everything for which I live, suffer from it, and it must cease. Will you lend me your aid in this?" But the famous preacher dismissed Woodhull's letter, calling it "whining."

After Beecher refused to help her, Woodhull decided to tell the world about the powerful preacher's private life. She began making speeches about Beecher's affairs. The money she earned for these speeches paid enough for her to restart her newspaper—at least briefly. In October 1872, *Woodhull & Claflin's Weekly* published a special edition—which came to be known as the "scandal" issue—detailing the preacher's affair with Elizabeth Tilton. Woodhull's newspaper story was true—but Woodhull and Claflin would pay a heavy price for their story.

Chapter Seven

Truth and Consequences

The *Weekly's* scandal issue hit newsstands on October 28, 1872. In addition to the news of Beecher's affair, the issue also included a story by Tennie about a Wall Street broker named Luther Challis. The article claimed that Challis had seduced two young women.

The newspaper sold for ten cents. But by nightfall, people were paying two dollars and fifty cents for a copy. The first ten thousand copies sold out quickly—everyone in town was talking about the *Weekly.* Those lucky enough to have an issue rented their newspapers to other readers for a dollar a day. One copy sold for forty dollars.

Three days later, U.S. marshals stopped a carriage carrying Woodhull and Claflin. The sisters had bundles of three thousand newspapers in the carriage. Law officers seized the papers and arrested the women, charging them with the crime of sending obscenity through the mail. The sisters had sent their newspaper to a man named Anthony Comstock, who had requested that his copy be mailed. When the paper arrived, Comstock alerted the authorities. Seeing himself as a protector of public morals, Comstock had purposely asked the women to send him the paper so that they would be charged with mailing obscene material. Then, under a new law that he himself had supported, Comstock and others could receive half of the fines paid by people arrested on obscenity charges.

The government took the charges against the sisters seriously. A top court official noted, "An example is needed and we propose to make one of these women." Bail was set at eight thousand dollars for each sister. (Bail is money that people who are arrested must pay to be released from jail before their case goes to court.) Noah Davis, the government's lawyer against the sisters, was a member of Beecher's congregation and a distant relative of the famous preacher. Shortly after the sisters were arrested and long before a trial that would decide whether or not they were guilty, Davis told a reporter that Woodhull and her sister, "have been guilty of a most . . . unjust charge against one of the purest and best citizens of this State."

While the sisters sat in jail, police searched the *Weekly* offices, seizing and destroying the presses used to print the newspaper. Colonel Blood and several newspaper staffers were arrested. The sisters' lawyer recommended that they not pay bail to get out of jail. The lawyer said that the government would simply rearrest them as soon as they went free. So Woodhull, Claflin, and Blood stayed in jail. The staffers who worked to print the sisters' newspaper, however, were able to pay bail and leave.

Noah Davis *(right)* was the prosecutor in the Woodhull-Claflin obscenity case. The case charged the women with sending indecent materials through the mail. Davis was a relative of Beecher, and he presumed the women guilty.

November 5, 1872, was election day. Voters across the country headed to the polls to choose their next president. Victoria Woodhull was still in jail. But Susan B. Anthony made history when she cast her ballot in Rochester, New York. She was arrested and found guilty but refused to pay the fine. Anthony is credited with being the first woman in the United States to vote—even though women wouldn't receive the right to vote for years to come. As for Woodhull, she would not have seen her name on the ballot even if she had been free. She hadn't been able to pay the necessary fees—and at thirty-four, she was still one year younger than the minimum age set in the Constitution for presidents. Still, twenty-two states had official delegates who intended to vote for the Equal Rights Party.

Most voters chose President Ulysses S. Grant. In response, Woodhull proposed that Grant be brought to trial for illegally acting as president when half of the country's citizens weren't allowed to vote. But she didn't have the power to have her plan taken seriously.

From jail Woodhull wrote to the *New York Herald* asking to be treated fairly. Many newspapers reprinted

In this engraving, Claflin and Woodhull *(sitting left)* meet with supporters in a New York City jail during their obscenity trial of 1872. But even from jail, Woodhull continued the fight for her cause.

Woodhull's letter. Beyond this move, however, Woodhull's fellow publishers did little to help or defend her.

After a month in jail, Woodhull and Claflin went free when two supporters paid their bail. But as their lawyer predicted, the sisters were soon arrested again. This time, they faced charges for the article Tennie had written about Luther Challis. Challis accused the sisters of libel (writing false information about another person that hurts his or her reputation). Once more, Woodhull and her sister were jailed and later bailed out.

Being in jail inspired Woodhull to write a new lecture, titled "Moral Cowardice and Modern Hypocrisy." She wanted to introduce the lecture in Boston—the Beechers' hometown—but city officials refused to let her speak. Instead, on December 20, 1872, Woodhull drew a crowd in nearby Springfield, Massachusetts.

Soon afterward, she drew bigger crowds at New York's Cooper Institute for another talk, called "The Naked Truth." Woodhull went to the lecture knowing the authorities would be there to arrest her. Law enforcement had already gone to the *Weekly* office and arrested Colonel Blood, but Woodhull wasn't there. Anthony Comstock was again the force behind Woodhull's arrest. Using a fake name, Comstock had copies of the scandal issue mailed to him in Connecticut. Woodhull stayed in hiding until it came time for her to give the speech. She spoke to the audience about spending time in jail, about Anthony Comstock and the government's efforts to shut down her paper and keep her from speaking out. After the speech, she went to jail—this time, for sending obscene material across state lines. Woodhull and Claflin would each end up facing eight charges for the same alleged crime—printing or mailing the October 28 scandal issue of the *Weekly*. But they were never charged with libeling Henry Ward Beecher. Many people knew that what the *Weekly* printed about the famous preacher and his affairs was true.

More than three months after the sisters were first arrested, prominent people began to come to their defense. Woodhull's ally in Congress, U.S. representative Benjamin Butler, wrote a letter supporting them in the *New York Sun*. The *Troy Whig and Daily Press* was the first newspaper to stand up on Woodhull's behalf. The paper wrote, "Through Victoria Woodhull and Tennie Claflin, American law has been outraged, the rights of the press assaulted, freedom of speech endangered and the functions of republican government usurped [seized] to cloak [protect] the reputation of one or two prominent individuals." Not surprisingly, Woodhull's reputation suffered after her numerous arrests. She was not invited to attend the 1873 suffrage convention.

In May 1873, the sisters had a new employee. They had hired Joseph Treat to edit and run the *Weekly* while they were busy with other matters. That month the *Weekly* reprinted the Beecher story. By then Beecher, Tilton, and Henry Bowen (a third Plymouth Church leader) were each accusing one another of serious wrongdoing. Bowen was the publisher of several religious newspapers, including the ones for which Tilton and Beecher wrote. Bowen's wife had confessed on her deathbed that she'd had an affair with Beecher.

The public grew suspicious about all the charges against Beecher. To defend their brother, two of Beecher's sisters, Catharine and Harriet, went on the attack. Catharine called Woodhull "insane," while Harriet described the suffragist publisher as a "vile jailbird." Another Beecher sister, Isabella Beecher Hooker, stood by Woodhull. Isabella, Woodhull's closest friend in the suffrage movement, asked her brother Henry if the adultery charges were true. He wrote back telling her to be silent. Thomas Beecher also thought

Isabella Beecher in the late 1800s. Isabella supported Woodhull and even asked her brother Henry Ward Beecher if Woodhull's reports of his infidelity were true. Isabella's sisters Harriet and Catharine, however, attacked Woodhull's character and state of mind.

his brother Henry was guilty. Thomas wrote Isabella, "Woodhull is my hero, and Henry my coward."

Elizabeth Cady Stanton told Isabella Beecher Hooker that she knew Woodhull was in the right. "I have not a shadow of doubt of the truth," she wrote firmly. "There is too much money locked up in Beecher's success for him to be sacrificed. The public, especially those who have a financial interest in this matter, would rather see every woman in the nation sacrificed than one of their idols of gold."

The May 17, 1873, *Weekly* was devoted entirely to the sisters' defense. In June 1873, eight months after the scandal issue was published, the sisters went on

A jury found Woodhull *(left)* and Claflin not guilty of the obscenity charges against them in June 1873.

trial. They had printed serious charges against one of the country's most influential men. And although the women wrote the truth, they ended up in jail and in debt defending themselves. The jury listened to the government's weak case against Woodhull and Claflin, and then the jury found the sisters not guilty. But even that joyful verdict couldn't repair the damage that had been done to Victoria and Tennie. As Woodhull later wrote, "exposing the Beecher scandal has been the shadow which has obscured everything that I did or said. . . . I had no idea in the beginning of the battle I was waging."

Following the trial, Woodhull filed a request asking the government to pay her and Tennie back for the money they had lost due to the many false charges. It would take time for the government to rule on that issue. For the time being, Woodhull's family continued to make news. Victoria and Tennie's sister Utica was arrested in June for disturbing the peace. Utica told police that Woodhull and Blood had beaten her. A month later, thirty-one-year-old Utica died after drinking too much.

Despite her personal problems, Woodhull continued to work toward public goals. That fall she spoke at the spiritualists' convention about "scarecrows of social freedom." By "scarecrows," Woodhull meant topics that distracted the public from serious issues. She wanted the public to think about reform—but instead, they focused on her family's problems, and on the sexual affairs of public figures such as herself or Beecher. While Woodhull herself had brought

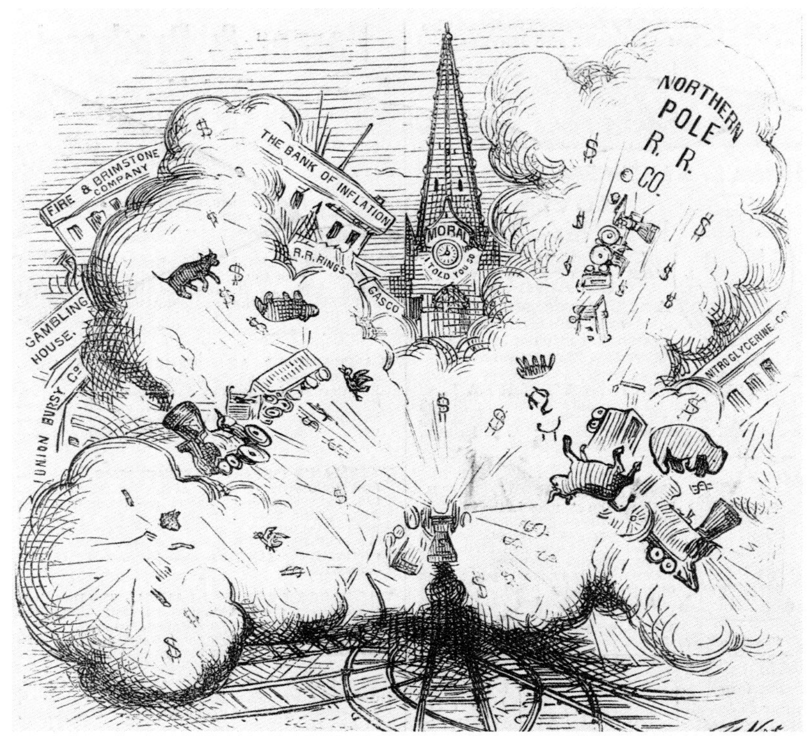

This editorial cartoon from 1873 illustrates the stock market crash of that year. Many people lost money, jobs, and businesses. Woodhull and Claflin were hit too and had to close their brokerage.

Beecher's affair to light, she believed the time had come to focus on bigger issues.

Before long, the public was forced to pay attention to serious matters. The country's weak economy collapsed on September 18, 1873. More than two dozen New York bank and Wall Street brokerage firms failed. The stock market plunged, and President Grant ordered that no stocks could be traded for ten days to give the country time to stabilize. But the country continued to suffer. Within months, five thousand businesses closed. Thousands of workers lost their jobs, and farmers lost their land. Woodhull and Claflin's brokerage company had to shut down.

Woodhull continued to write and lecture. The weeks in jail and the years of continued controversy, along with a draining travel schedule, left her exhausted and sick. Her lungs ached from riding on smoky, coal-powered trains and using her voice night after night in crowded auditoriums. But Woodhull couldn't afford to stop speaking. She earned $280 per lecture. Her income supported her children, husband, parents, and sister. Accompanied by her sister and husband, Woodhull spent most of 1874 on the circuit, speaking 150 nights. She estimated that she spoke to about twenty-five thousand people in that one year. She lectured about the working poor, and about women forced to stay in marriages where they had no power. Woodhull also talked to women-only audiences about birth control, a topic considered too delicate to discuss openly at the time.

While Woodhull, Blood, and Claflin toured, Blood's brother George stayed in New York to manage the newspaper and to care for Woodhull's children. Meanwhile, Joseph Treat continued to edit the *Weekly*. Some historians believe that he was in love with Victoria but that she did not return his attention. For whatever reasons, Treat soon turned against his boss. He even published a pamphlet that called her "the greatest fraud in the world." As Woodhull toured, Treat's pamphlets were handed to people outside the lecture halls. In response, Blood sued Treat for libel, but Treat died before a trial could take place.

In March 1874, the sisters were back in a New York courtroom, this time, facing the Challis libel charges. On the ninth day of the criminal trial, the jury found the women not guilty. The judge was furious. He called the jury's decision "the most outrageous verdict ever recorded." And although the Challis case later went to another court, neither sister was ever found guilty of any obscenity or libel charge.

This editorial illustration from 1875 depicts testimony from the Beecher-Tilton case. In addition to images of Beecher's infidelity, one image hints at a Woodhull-Tilton affair *(upper left)*.

Then, in January 1875, Congress denied Woodhull's request to pay her and Tennie back for the money they lost because of their many arrests. But the story of Beecher's adultery continued to play out in court. Theodore Tilton sued Beecher for ruining the Tiltons' marriage. The trial in the Beecher-Tilton scandal, as it was known, made headlines for two years. Woodhull didn't have to testify, but the court did order her to show letters she had written to Theodore Tilton. The case ended in July 1875 after the jury failed to agree on a verdict. The case was closed, and Beecher was free to go. The leaders of Plymouth Church stood behind their famous minister, even raising one hundred thousand dollars to pay his legal fees. In the end, the Reverend Henry Ward Beecher lost very little. Theodore Tilton, however, was financially destroyed.

A year later, on June 10, 1876, Woodhull published the final issue of her *Weekly*. The newspaper had survived six years and had made a major impression. Blood didn't want the paper to fold, but Woodhull was tired. She wanted to stop lecturing. She wanted to stop traveling all over the country. She wanted to be seen as respectable.

In September 1876, Woodhull resigned as president of the spiritualists' association. Her last big power base was gone. That same month, she filed for divorce from Blood, claiming he had committed adultery (had affairs with other women). At that time, courts usually would not allow a woman to divorce her husband unless he had been unfaithful.

However, adultery probably wasn't the real reason their marriage ended. Victoria Woodhull was tired and wanted a different kind of life. And part of changing her life was ending her marriage to Colonel Blood. The divorce was granted on October 8, 1876. Blood said, "The grandest woman in the world went back on me."

Chapter Eight
New Country, New Life

On January 4, 1877, Cornelius Vanderbilt died. His children argued over the one hundred million dollars' worth of property and savings that he left behind—a sum roughly equal to all the money in the U.S. Treasury. William Vanderbilt stood to receive the bulk of his father's inheritance, but his siblings sued to get what they saw as their fair share. William was worried that the court overseeing how Vanderbilt's estate was divided might ask Woodhull and Claflin to testify. The sisters' testimony about Vanderbilt's belief in spirits might make the railroad tycoon seem unstable. Vanderbilt's will would only be followed if he was believed to have been in good mental health. And Tennie Claflin, as Vanderbilt's longtime companion, also was fighting to get her own share of the Vanderbilt fortune. So William Vanderbilt offered Woodhull and Claflin more than one hundred thousand dollars if they would leave the country.

The sisters took the money and set sail for Great Britain in August 1877. Traveling with their mother, Victoria's children, and servants, they went first class. Woodhull said she left the United States to make a better life for Zula. "I have a fair daughter just budding into womanhood, to whom I wish to leave an untarnished name," she explained. "[I leave] for her sake, much more than for my own." They settled in England, which was then ruled by Queen Victoria, the long-serving monarch for whom Woodhull had been named decades earlier. But even in Great Britain, Victoria and Tennie could not seem to escape scandals and gossip. Their reputations followed them across the Atlantic. Claflin wrote to her father that "the lies, slanders & filth were worse here than even in America. It got so bad the air was poisoned."

Despite the rumors, Woodhull tried to work. Energized by time to rest and a new country, Woodhull launched another lecture, called "The Human Body: The Temple of God." The *Nottingham Guardian* wrote, "Mrs. Woodhull is unquestionably a great orator [speaker], and it is not difficult to understand how she has gained so remarkable a hold upon the people of her own country." Woodhull's speaking tour, which began in Nottingham in September, proceeded to Liverpool and Manchester before ending in London. At the London talk in December, a wealthy banker named John Biddulph Martin heard Woodhull for the first time.

Martin's family had controlled a major bank in Great Britain for five generations. The tall, dark-haired bachelor had won many trophies as a runner while studying at Oxford University. Yet despite his good looks, money, and talents, Martin was not content. Four years earlier, his younger sister Penelope

Woodhull *(right)* and Claflin moved to England in 1877. Woodhull continued to give lectures and to publish her suffragist literature.

had died in childbirth. She had been his closest friend. Penelope was a suffragist who wrote anonymous essays championing women's rights. Martin had his sister's work published.

After hearing Woodhull's lecture, Martin wanted to talk with the outspoken suffragist. The two met once, but it would be another year before they saw each other again. After that second meeting, the established British banker soon began paying visits to the controversial American. Later, he would tell a friend that Woodhull "was more alive than anyone I have ever met. Ordinary words don't describe her. When you were with her everything became so thrilling, so worthwhile."

Woodhull didn't want to repeat the chaotic lifestyle she had had in the United States. In England she tried to make her life—past and present—seem tamer. She wrote a series of "Life Sketches," articles that gave a whitewashed version of her biography. She started using the name Woodhall, which she said dated back to her English ancestors. She renounced many of her former beliefs, saying, "During no part of my life did I favor free love."

Yet even as Woodhull tried to tone down her colorful past, details continued to surface. In 1878 Elizabeth Tilton publicly admitted that she and Henry Ward Beecher had had a relationship. Henry Bowen

In 1878 Elizabeth Tilton *(left)* confessed to her affair with Henry Ward Beecher. Henry Bowen also admitted that his wife had had an affair with the minister, further validating Woodhull's early reports.

revealed that his late wife had an affair with the famous preacher. The news reminded people of Woodhull's role in publicizing Beecher's affairs and her time in jail.

When Martin and Woodhull became more serious, he began to hear from people about Woodhull's past. Woodhull offered a reward to anyone who could prove who was spreading lies about her. But Martin didn't seem to be swayed by the rumors. He and Woodhull continue to spend time together. He rented the house next to Woodhull's. In December 1880, the couple became engaged.

Woodhull went to New York to try to stop the rumors that continued to swirl about her. While she was in the city, she saw James Blood on the street. Woodhull walked past her former husband without a word, while he nearly fainted. The two would never see each other again.

On October 31, 1883, Woodhull and Martin quietly married. Woodhull's family attended the small church service, but no one from the groom's family was there. Martin's brother, Richard, said that Woodhull was trying to grab the family's money. He swore that he would not welcome her in his home. But eventually, Martin's parents did agree to meet their son's new wife.

The couple's marriage certificate included a blank space for Woodhull's occupation. It wasn't clear what she would do after marrying Martin. For a time, she simply settled into her new life. A few months after their wedding, the newlyweds bought a mansion in

Woodhull and her husband John moved to London's Hyde Park neighborhood *(above)* in 1883.

Hyde Park, an elegant neighborhood in London. They lived happily, spending much time together in the home they called their "dear nest." Their next few years passed quietly. It was the first time in decades that Victoria Woodhull was out of the public eye.

Two years after Woodhull married a wealthy Englishman, her sister Tennessee did the same. In October 1885, Tennie wed Francis Cook. Cook had built an impressive concert hall to honor the Princess of Wales. Queen Victoria rewarded Cook by making him a baronet (a member of British nobility). That meant that Tennie became Lady Cook. The sisters had once been poor, sometimes jailed, and often controversial.

They had faced countless rumors in their native country. Yet they were now part of Britain's high society. Cook and Martin ran newspaper ads offering rewards for the conviction of anyone who tried to blackmail their wives.

To further protect his wife's reputation, Martin hired a detective to search for James Blood. Woodhull blamed her ex-husband for spreading rumors about her. But Blood had actually tried to defend his former wife, writing articles and essays to counter the rumors about her. Martin's detective found that Blood had remarried. He had then gone to western Africa, where he died in December 1885.

As time went on, Woodhull began spending more and more time at home. She preferred her husband's company to the busy social life she'd once known. The couple wrote each other countless notes. One letter from Martin urged Woodhull to "be strong & brave, little wife, and trust in God and your husband whose love will bat down all that would do you evil."

Back in the United States, seventy-four-year-old Henry Ward Beecher had a stroke and died in 1887. His sister Isabella had rushed to his house. She hoped he would confess his sins and die with a clear conscience. Instead, Henry's wife refused to let Isabella see her brother. The stories about Beecher's affairs had almost destroyed Victoria Woodhull. Yet they had not dramatically changed Beecher's life. When he died, Henry Ward Beecher was still a popular minister.

Meanwhile, Woodhull wrote her autobiography. Although she published two, she never captured many details of her life on paper. Her writing does provide glimpses into how she saw herself. She wrote, "Shattered in health, reduced in pocket, almost heart-broken, she came to England, with the instinct of a wounded deer, to hide in solitude. Victoria Woodhull found the heart and the home of a great souled English gentleman open to receive her, and afford her a haven of rest and peace."

Woodhull seemed grateful for the quiet life she found in England with her husband. But she never lost her feelings for her homeland. Every July 4, to celebrate both their countries, Woodhull and Martin hosted Interdependence Day parties, decorating their home with intertwined flags of the United States and Great Britain.

The parties and sheltered life suited Woodhull for a time. But after a few quiet years, she was ready to go public again. In 1892 Woodhull began publishing the *Humanitarian, a Monthly Magazine of Sociology*. Once again, Woodhull researched and wrote on a range of issues, from politics to food safety.

Woodhull and Martin spent the spring of 1892 in New York City. While there, they launched the U.S. version of the *Humanitarian.* Later that year, Woodhull announced she was again running for president. Her first run for president in 1872 had been filled with passion and energy—and, in the end, no money. Twenty years later, Woodhull's passion was muted, but her bank account was full. John Martin paid to print and distribute an expensive leather-bound pamphlet detailing his wife's role in the suffrage movement.

The pamphlet went to each delegate at an 1892 meeting of the National American Woman Suffrage Association. The couple wanted to make sure that young delegates knew about Woodhull's contributions. Elizabeth Cady Stanton and Susan B. Anthony had written an 899-page history of the suffrage movement that barely mentioned Woodhull.

Woodhull's 1892 bid to be president of a country she no longer lived in was more about restoring her name than running her nation. But she still had many ideas. She wanted women to be better educated about the world so they could make a decent living. She wanted women to be better educated about their bodies so they could control their lives. She lectured in London about humanitarian government before returning to the United States, where audiences still seemed curious about her.

On May 8, 1892, the *Chicago Mail* reminded readers that Woodhull had broken the Henry Ward Beecher story. A reporter wrote, "All America knows that Victoria Woodhull was solely responsible for the greatest scandal of the century." Despite people's ongoing curiosity about her life, however, Woodhull knew that she didn't have any real chance of becoming president. Grover Cleveland was elected for a second term in 1892. Afterward, Woodhull commented, "To be perfectly frank, I hardly expected to be elected. The truth is I am too many years ahead of this age, and the exalted views and objects of humanitarianism can scarcely be grasped as yet by the unenlightened mind of the average man."

In 1893 Woodhull and her sister Tennessee had a fight over Tennie's husband. Woodhull didn't think Cook treated her sister very well. Historians do not know exactly what Victoria said to Tennie about the issue. Neither woman ever spoke publicly about what happened between them. But the result was clear: the two sisters, who had gone through tremendous highs and lows together, would never be close again.

Victoria herself ended up in court again in 1894. The Martins were suing the famous British Museum. They claimed that the museum had several materials that libeled Woodhull, including Joseph Treat's pamphlet. British newspapers happily covered the battle

Woodhull found herself back in court in 1894, suing the British Museum *(below)* for libel. The museum agreed to remove the materials that wrongfully marred her reputation.

between one of Britain's greatest museums and a wealthy official of one of the country's leading banks. The case went to court and ended with a mixed ruling. The Martins had to pay court costs, but the museum agreed to keep the offending material off the shelves.

Woodhull's next challenge involved her thirty-three-year-old daughter. Zula had fallen in love with an American. Her mother quickly went to the United States to persuade Zula not to marry. Woodhull was worried about who would watch over her son after she died. Although Byron was almost forty years old, his mental disabilities meant that he would always need someone to care for him. Woodhull wanted to make sure that Zula would protect Byron. Woodhull also worried that if Zula gave birth, her child might be disabled like Byron. Whatever Woodhull said to Zula worked. Zula didn't marry. She went home to England, instead, to be with her mother and brother.

Woodhull and Martin continued to enjoy their home and each other's companionship. But as they grew older, each faced health problems. John Martin's doctor suggested that the fifty-five-year-old banker go somewhere warmer to avoid London's chilly winter air. But Woodhull's own health kept her from traveling. Martin left for the Canary Islands (off the coast of northwestern Africa) alone. There, he fell while riding his bicycle in the mountains. He died on March 20, 1897, far from the wife he loved. In the May 1897 *Humanitarian,* Victoria wrote sweetly about her "unruffled and courteous" husband. She called him "a gentleman in the truest sense of the word."

Martin had been too far from home at the time of his accident to know that his elderly father had died just a few days earlier. So when Martin himself died, Woodhull inherited not only his estate but also his share of his father's property. By today's standards, Woodhull received about fourteen million dollars worth of land and money. The biggest piece of property Woodhull inherited was Bredon's Norton, a large country estate.

In 1901, at the age of sixty-three, Woodhull sold the *Humanitarian.* She left London to retire to the country at Bredon's Norton with her adult children. She and Zula decided to modernize the village by their estate. They installed streetlights and telephones and tore down old buildings. Later, the mother and daughter opened a school for the village children. The Woodhull women wanted to improve villagers' lives—but they never asked local people about what they wanted. Villagers ended up wrecking the new lights, and the model school closed just two years after it opened.

In 1901, when Tennie's husband died, Victoria tried to reconnect with her sister. "My darling blessed sister," Woodhull wrote. "I so long to come and see you. How is it that our lives cannot be brought together now in our few remaining years of life?" But Tennie never made peace with her sister.

Meanwhile, Woodhull turned her attention to a new passion. At the turn of the century, automobiles were playthings of the rich. Cars—the faster the better—fascinated Woodhull. She and Zula made history as

A woman drives a Pierce-Arrow in the early twentieth century. Woodhull was passionate about cars, as well as aircraft.

the first women to drive from England through France and back. The sixty-five-year-old widow was a proud member of the Ladies Automobile Club. She also helped organize the Women's Aerial League of Great Britain to promote the joys of airplanes. She even offered a reward to the first person to fly across the Atlantic Ocean.

Woodhull seemed content in her country estate. And gradually, she and the village adapted to one another. By 1911 Woodhull's former school building and grounds had found a new use as a community center. When World War I (1914–1918) began, Woodhull helped the Red Cross by hosting sewing parties and donating hats to the army. The massive war involved most of Europe and eventually the United States. Called the Great War, it was the largest conflict the world had ever seen. Four years of battles left about ten million people dead. During the war, Woodhull tried to make life easier for the people in her village. Resources of all kinds—from food to fuel—were limited. Woodhull donated vegetable seeds to the whole village so that people could grow their own food.

On January 18, 1923, Tennie died. Victoria and her sister had never mended their rift, although Tennie's last writings had included kind words about Wood-

Tennie Claflin *(seated right)* attends a suffragist meeting about one year before her death in 1923. Woodhull died four years later.

hull. But with Tennie gone, the only people close to Woodhull were her children. Nevertheless, Woodhull continued to make an impression on all those who knew her. On September 23, 1924—Woodhull's eighty-sixth birthday—the Bredon's Norton villagers put together a book that they all signed and dedicated to "Lady Bountiful," thanking her for everything she had done for the village.

On June 9, 1927, Victoria C. Woodhull died. She was eighty-eight years old. Woodhull's ashes were scattered in the Atlantic Ocean, between Great Britain and America, the two countries she loved. She had been born poor in the United States, where she used her brains and ambition to gain a fortune. She ran for president decades before women had the right to vote but spent election day in jail. In her new home across the ocean, Woodhull found love and some peace and quiet, but she never forgot where she came from or what she had accomplished. She was a woman ahead of her time. Now—her life is a part of history.

In Her Own Words

Victoria Woodhull made history in January 1871 when she became the first woman to speak before Congress. She asked for the right to vote. One month later, when Congress denied women that right, Woodhull made another speech. At Lincoln Hall in Washington, D.C., Woodhull told her audience that women were living under the same kind of oppression—taxation without representation—that led American colonists to revolt against Britain in the 1700s.

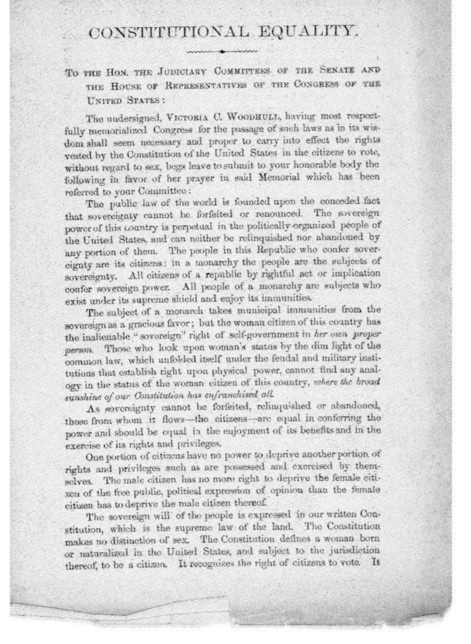

CONSTITUTIONAL EQUALITY.

To the Hon. the Judiciary Committees of the Senate and the House of Representatives of the Congress of the United States:

The undersigned, Victoria C. Woodhull, having most respectfully memorialized Congress for the passage of such laws as in its wisdom shall seem necessary and proper to carry into effect the rights vested by the Constitution of the United States in the citizens to vote, without regard to sex, begs leave to submit to your honorable body the following in favor of her prayer in said Memorial which has been referred to your Committee:

The public law of the world is founded upon the conceded fact that sovereignty cannot be forfeited or renounced. The sovereign power of this country is perpetual in the politically-organized people of the United States, and can neither be relinquished nor abandoned by any portion of them. The people in this Republic who confer sovereignty are its citizens: in a monarchy the people are the subjects of sovereignty. All citizens of a republic by rightful act or implication confer sovereign power. All people of a monarchy are subjects who exist under its supreme shield and enjoy its immunities.

The subject of a monarch takes municipal immunities from the sovereign as a gracious favor; but the woman citizen of this country has the inalienable "sovereign" right of self-government in *her own proper person.* Those who look upon woman's status by the dim light of the common law, which unfolded itself under the feudal and military institutions that establish right upon physical power, cannot find any analogy in the status of the woman citizen of this country, *where the broad sunshine of our Constitution has enfranchised all.*

As sovereignty cannot be forfeited, relinquished or abandoned, those from whom it flows—the citizens—are equal in conferring the power and should be equal in the enjoyment of its benefits and in the exercise of its rights and privileges.

One portion of citizens have no power to deprive another portion of rights and privileges such as are possessed and exercised by themselves. The male citizen has no more right to deprive the female citizen of the free public, political expression of opinion than the female citizen has to deprive the male citizen thereof.

The sovereign will of the people is expressed in our written Constitution, which is the supreme law of the land. The Constitution makes no distinction of sex. The Constitution defines a woman born or naturalized in the United States, and subject to the jurisdiction thereof, to be a citizen. It recognizes the right of citizens to vote. It

The 1871 record of Woodhull's speech to Congress

Woodhull also compared women to slaves. After the Civil War, Congress passed the Fifteenth Amendment. The amendment granted voting rights to all adult male citizens, including freed African American slaves. Woodhull ended her speech (excerpted below) by saying that if women weren't given the vote, they should revolt and form their own government.

> I make the plain and broad assertion, that the women of this country are as much subject to men as the slaves were to their masters.

. . . If the male negroes, as citizens possessed the right to vote, shall it be assumed that women citizens do not possess the same right?. . .

If the right to vote shall not be denied to any person of any race, how shall it be denied to the female part of all races? Even if it could be denied on account of sex, I ask, what warrant men have to presume that it is the female sex to whom such denial can be made instead of the male sex? Men, you are wrong, and you stand convicted before the world of denying me, a woman, the right to vote, not by any right of law, but simply because you have usurped [stolen] the power so to do, just as all other tyrants in all ages have, to rule their subjects. . . .

For men to say to women, "You shall not vote because you are women" is intolerable; is unbearable, and it will not do for Congress to quietly allow this disenfranchisement [lack of voting power] to continue. . . .

Under such glaring inconsistencies, such unwarrantable tyranny, such unscrupulous despotism [unfair leadership], what is there left [for] women to do but to become the mothers of the future government?. . .

We mean treason; we mean secession, and on a thousand times grander scale than was that of the South [during the Civil War]. We are plotting revolution.

THE FIGHT FOR RIGHTS

Victoria Woodhull was not the first American woman to run for public office. Elizabeth Cady Stanton had run unsuccessfully for U.S. Congress in 1866. Woodhull's candidacy was also a long shot. But when the Civil War had ended in 1865, many people had assumed that both African Americans and women would quickly gain more rights. In 1870 Congress had indeed passed the Fifteenth Amendment, which granted African American men the right to vote. Women still lacked that right, however, and suffragists renewed their fight for the vote.

In 1917 a new movement began that led to action. During President Woodrow Wilson's term in office (1913–1921), a group of suffragists known as the Silent Sentinels launched a peaceful protest outside the White House. Beginning on January 10,

A suffragist demonstrates outside the White House in Washington, D.C., in 1917.

Suffragist leader Alice Paul *(right)* led the Sentinels' protest for women's right to vote. The protest was held outside the White House from 1917 to 1918.

more than one thousand women holding signs and banners gathered outside the president's residence. Their signs displayed slogans including "Democracy Should Begin at Home" and "Mr. President how long must women wait for liberty."

Led by suffragist leader Alice Paul, the Sentinels continued their protest six days a week, for eighteen months. Some of the women were arrested. Others were shouted at and even physically attacked by onlookers. Still they kept up their efforts. When Alice Paul was arrested and sent to prison, she began a hunger strike, refusing to eat in order to protest her treatment. Other imprisoned suffragists joined her. In response, prison guards abused the women, beating some of them severely.

Suffragists march for the vote in New York City. The banner they are carrying proclaims President Woodrow Wilson's support of the suffragist cause in the early 1900s.

As word of this violence spread, more and more people began taking the side of the suffragists. At last, on January 9, 1918, President Woodrow Wilson announced that he would support the Nineteenth Amendment. On January 10—two years after the Sentinels began their protest—the U.S. House of Representatives passed the amendment. It seemed as though victory was near, but the Senate then delayed its vote on the issue. When the senators did vote in October, the amendment failed to pass by just two votes.

Unwilling to give up the progress that the suffragists had gained so far, the National Woman's Party

(NWP) took action. The NWP was a women's rights organization that focused on fighting for the Nineteenth Amendment. When elections for the U.S. Senate were held in the fall of 1918, the NWP encouraged citizens to vote against candidates who had opposed suffrage. As a result, the next time the amendment came up for a vote, most senators were pro-suffrage. The amendment was passed by the House on May 21, 1919. On June 4, it was passed by the Senate. And on August 18, 1920, the Nineteenth Amendment was ratified and became law.

Victoria Woodhull's dream had come true. Forty-eight years after she first ran for president, she finally saw U.S. women win the right to vote.

The Nineteenth Amendment reads:

Section 1. The right of citizens of the United States to vote shall not be denied or abridged [limited] by the United States or by any State on account of sex.

Section 2. Congress shall have power to enforce this article by appropriate legislation.

Source Notes

9 Barbara Goldsmith, *Other Powers: The Age of Suffrage, Spiritualism and the Scandalous Victoria Woodhull* (New York: Alfred A. Knopf, 1998), 192.
11 Lois Beachy Underhill, *The Woman Who Ran for President: The Many Lives of Victoria Woodhull* (Bridgehampton, NY: Bridge Works Publishing, 1995), 12.
12 Goldsmith, 25.
12 Jacqueline McLean, *Victoria Woodhull: First Woman Presidential Candidate,* (Greensboro, NC: Morgan Reynolds, 2000), 14.
12 Goldsmith, 25.
15 McLean, 20.
15 Goldsmith, 52.
15 McLean, 22.
16 Mary Gabriel, *Notorious Victoria* (Chapel Hill: Algonquin Books of Chapel Hill, 1998), 14.
17 Goldsmith, 65.
17 Gabriel, 16.
18 Underhill, 27.
18 Goldsmith, 67.
18 Underhill, 31.
18–19 Goldsmith, 67.
21 Underhill, 29.
21 McLean, 26.
22 Underhill, 32.
22 McLean, 30.
22 Underhill, 37.
26 McLean, 35.
26 Ibid.
29 Underhill, 52.
29 Gabriel, 39.
31 Underhill, 59.
32 Goldsmith, 193.
32 Gabriel, 2.

32 Ibid., 42.
32–34 Underhill, 68.
35 Goldsmith, 195.
36 Underhill, 8.
36 Ibid., 77.
37–38 Gabriel, 56.
38 Underhill, 86.
38 Ibid.
41 Gabriel, 66.
42–43 Goldsmith, 250.
43 Ibid.
43 Underhill, 99.
44 Gabriel, 76.
44 Underhill, 104.
44 Ibid.
47 Gabriel, 96.
48 Ibid., 97.
48 Ibid., 91–92.
48–49 Gabriel, 100.
50 Underhill, 143.
50 Ibid., 144.
52 Ibid., 127.
55 McLean, 66.
56 Ibid.
56 Ibid.
56 Ibid.
57 Underhill, 185.
58 Ibid., 194.
58 Ibid., 200.
48–59 Amanda Frisken, *Victoria Woodhull's Sexual Revolution: Political Theater and the Popular Press in Nineteenth-Century America* (Philadelphia: University of Pennsylvania Press, 2004), 46.
60 Gabriel, 171.
63 Underhill, 218.
64 Ibid., 214.
65 Gabriel, 176.

65 Ibid., 177.
68 Underhill, 230.
68 Ibid.
72 Ibid., 237.
73 Ibid., 241.
74 Ibid., 245.
74 Ibid., 247.
75 Ibid., 227.
75 Gabriel, 214.
77 Underhill, 264.
78 Gabriel, 228.
80 Underhill, 273.
82 Ibid.
82 Gabriel, 246.
82 McLean, 90.
83 Underhill, 280.
84 Ibid., 283.
86 Ibid., 286.
87 Gabriel, 263.
88 Ibid., 264.
89 Goldsmith, 6.
89 Underhill, 294.
91 Ibid., 300–301.
92 Ibid., 301.
95 McLean, 102.
96–97 Victoria Woodhull, "A Lecture on Constitutional Equality," *Library of Congress: American Memory,* n.d., http://memory.loc.gov/cgi-bin/query/r?ammem/naw:@field(DOCID+@lit(rbnawsan1569div1)) (March 9, 2006).
99 Wikipedia contributors, "Silent Sentinels," *Wikipedia: The Free Encyclopedia,* January 23, 2006, http://en.wikipedia.org/wiki/ Silent_Sentinels (March 9, 2006).
99 "Constitution of the United States, Amendments 11–27," *The National Archives Experience,* n.d., http://www.archives.gov/national-archives-experience/charters/constitution_amendments_11-27.html (March 9, 2006).

Selected Bibliography

Brinkley, Douglas. *American Heritage History of the United States.* New York: Viking, 1998.

"Constitution of the United States, Amendments 11–27." *The National Archives Experience.* N.d., http://www.archives.gov/national-archives-experience/charters/constitution_amendments_11-27.html (March 9, 2006).

Frisken, Amanda. *Victoria Woodhull's Sexual Revolution: Political Theater and the Popular Press in Nineteenth-Century America.* Philadelphia: University of Pennsylvania Press, 2004.

Gabriel, Mary. *Notorious Victoria.* Chapel Hill, NC: Algonquin Books of Chapel Hill, 1998.

Goldsmith, Barbara. *Other Powers: The Age of Suffrage, Spiritualism and the Scandalous Victoria Woodhull.* New York: Alfred A. Knopf, 1998.

Holland, Barbara. *They Went Whistling: Women Wayfarers, Warriors, Runaways, and Renegades.* New York: Pantheon Books, 2001.

McLean, Jacqueline. *Victoria Woodhull: First Woman Presidential Candidate.* Greensboro, NC: Morgan Reynolds, 2000.

New York Times Company, the. *New York Times on the Web.* 2005. http://www.nytimes.com (December 14, 2005).

Taylor, Tim. *The Book of Presidents.* New York: Arno Press, 1972.

Underhill, Lois Beachy. *The Woman Who Ran for President: The Many Lives of Victoria Woodhull.* Bridgehampton, NY: Bridge Works Publishing, 1995.

Ward, Geoffrey C. *The Civil War: An Illustrated History.* With Ric Burns and Ken Burns. New York: Alfred A. Knopf, 1990.

Ware, Susan, ed. *Forgotten Heroes: Inspiring American Portraits from Our Leading Historians.* New York: The Free Press, 1998.

Wikipedia contributors. "Silent Sentinels." *Wikipedia: The Free Encyclopedia.* January 23, 2006. http://en.wikipedia.org/wiki/Silent_Sentinels (March 9, 2006).

Woodhull, Victoria. "A Lecture on Constitutional Equality." *Library of Congress: American Memory.* N.d. http://memory.loc.gov/cgi-bin/query/r?ammem/naw:@field(DOCID+@lit(rbnawsan1569div1)(March 9, 2006).

Other Resources

Books

Adams, Colleen. *Women's Suffrage: A Primary Source History of the Women's rights Movement in America.* New York: Rosen Central Primary Source, 2003.

Adiletta, Dawn C. *Elizabeth Cady Stanton: Women's Suffrage and the First Vote.* New York: Rosen/PowerPlus Books, 2005.

Banfield, Susan. *The Fifteenth Amendment: African-American Men's Right to Vote.* Springfield, NJ: Enslow, 1998.

Bausum, Ann. *Our Country's Presidents.* Washington, DC: National Geographic Society, 2001.

Donovan, Sandy. *Running for Office: A Look at Political Campaigns.* Minneapolis: Lerner Publications Company, 2004.

Dumbeck, Kristina. *Leaders of Women's Suffrage.* San Diego: Lucent Books, 2000.

Fritz, Jean. *Harriet Beecher Stowe and the Beecher Preachers.* New York: Scholastic, 1994.

Gaughen, Shasta, ed. *Women's Rights.* San Diego: Greenhaven Press, 2003.

Greene, Meg. *Into the Land of Freedom: African Americans in Reconstruction.* Minneapolis: Lerner Publications Company, 2004.

Gulotta, Charles. *Extraordinary Women in Politics.* New York: Children's Press, 1999.

Havelin, Kate. *Ulysses S. Grant.* Minneapolis: Lerner Publications Company, 2004.

Kendall, Martha E. *Failure Is Impossible! The History of American Women's Rights.* Minneapolis: Twenty-First Century Books, 2001.

Miller, Brandon Marie. *Good Women of a Well-Bless Land: Women's Lives in Colonial America.* Minneapolis: Lerner Publications Company, 2003.

Monroe, Judy. *The Nineteenth Amendment: Women's Right to Vote.* Springfield, NJ: Enslow Publishers, 1998.

St. George, Judith, and David Small. *So You Want to Be President?* New York: Philomel, 2000.

Thimmesh, Catherine. *Madam President.* Boston: Houghton Mifflin, 2004.

Websites

Anthony Center for Women's Leadership: History of Women's Suffrage
http://www.rochester.edu/SBA/history.html
Find a wealth of information on the suffrage movement.

National Women's Hall of Fame
http://www.greatwomen.org
Browse biographies of remarkable women, including Victoria Woodhull. (Link to her biography by visiting http://www.greatwomen.org/women.php?action=viewone&id=196.)

Victoria Woodhull
http://www.nwhp.org/tlp/biographies/woodhull/woodhull_bio.html
This site from the National Women's History Project presents a timeline of Victoria Woodhull's life.

Victoria Woodhull, the Spirit to Run the White House
http://www.victoria-woodhull.com
This site from Victoria Woodhull & Company is a clearinghouse of information, including archival stories from *Woodhull & Claflin's Weekly,* the 1872 Woodhull campaign song, a student section, and more.

Index

Author Biography

Kate Havelin is a writer, runner, and political activist who lives in Saint Paul, Minnesota, with her husband and two sons. She is active in grassroots advocacy groups, including the Million Mom March, a group concerned with gun violence. She has run ten marathons and written fourteen books for young people, plus one running trails guidebook for adults.

Photo Acknowledgments

The images in this book are used with the permission of: © Hulton Archive/Getty Images, pp. 2, 33, 64; © Brown Brothers, pp. 7, 28 (both), 51, 54, 84, 90; © Mary Evans Picture Library, pp. 8, 49; © Rischgitz/Getty Images, p.10; © North Wind Picture Archives, p. 13; Library of Congress, pp. 14 (LC-USZ62-134484), 19 (LC-USZ62-91048), 20 (LC-USZ62-105413), 23 (LC-USZ62-67848), 24 (LC-USZ62-134029), 27 (LC-USZC2-2531), 29 (LC-DIG-ggbain-12783), 30 (LC-USZ62-67999), 31 (LC-USZC4-2461), 34 , 37 (LC-USZ62-97946), 40 (LC-DIG-cwpbh-01343), 44 (LC-USZ62-2023), 53 (LC-USZC2-782), 57 (LC-USZ62-16530), 59 (LC-USZ62-101054), 62 (LC-USZ62-89735), 69 (LC-DIG-cwpbh-00620), 73 (LC-USZ62-102765), 76 (LC-USZ62-119782), 78 (LC-USZ62-121959), 86 (LC-DIG-ppmsc-08574), 93 (LC-USZ62-19394), 94 (LC-USZ62-45807), 96, 98, 99 (LC-USZ62-37937), 100 (LC-USZ62-38965); Heritage Auction Galleries, p. 38 ; © The Art Archive/Culver Pictures, p. 46; © The Granger Collection, New York, p. 70; © Bettmann/CORBIS, pp. 74, 83.

Front cover: © Bettmann/CORBIS.
Front cover background: Heritage Auction Galleries